A Roadmap to Financial Freedom:

Simplify Your Finances, Secure Your Future, and Empower Generation

Kevin M. Gutirrez

Table of Contents

Introduction:

In a world where financial stability and independence are vital for personal success, "A road map to financial freedom" digs into the depths of financial intelligence to equip readers with the information, tools, and mentality required to master the art of saving. This engaging and thorough book goes beyond surface-level advice and provides a holistic approach to financial smartness, allowing people to acquire actual control over their money and pave the route to a safe and successful future.

1. What is financial freedom

Financial freedom is a state of being in which a person has the financial means and flexibility to live life on their own terms without being bound by money-related worries. It often entails having enough assets, investments, or passive income streams to meet one's living expenditures, allowing for options such as early retirement, following one's hobbies, or taking chances without fear of financial insecurity. Financial independence may mean various things to different individuals; it depends on what financial freedom means to you. It might mean retiring early, touring the globe, launching your dream company, or just living a stress-free life without financial concerns. Our journey starts with you determining what financial independence means to you. Throughout this book, your definition will serve as your guidepost.

2. Establishing your financial goal

Defining your financial ideal Setting financial objects is a critical first step toward financial success and security. Then is a step- by- step strategy to establishing financial objects

1. Specify your thing First, consider your financial guiding principles and pretensions. What are your financial pretensions, and why are they important to you? Consider your short- and long- term pretensions.

2. Set specific financial and non-financial pretensions. rather than simply saying," I want to save further plutocrat," be precise about how much, when, and why. Consider the statement," I want to save$ 10,000 for a down payment on a house within the coming two times."

3. Classify Your pretensions Divide your pretensions into several orders, similar as-Short-term pretensions(for the coming one to two

times) -Long- term pretensions(3- 5 times) -Long- term pretensions(10 times or further, similar as withdrawal)

4. Prioritize: Determine which objectives are most essential to you. Not all objectives are created equal, and you may need to prioritize one before pursuing others. Consider what will have the largest influence on your life.

5. Quantify Your Objectives: Assign exact figures and timelines to your objectives. This makes them quantifiable and time-bound, allowing you to measure progress.

6. Consider Your present status: Evaluate your present financial status. What are your assets and debts? What are your income, spending, and savings rate? Understanding your financial situation is essential for planning.

7. Consider Inflation and Returns: When planning long-term objectives, consider inflation and predicted investment returns. This ensures

that your objectives are realistic and take into account the changing worth of money.

8. Create an emergency fund before pursuing other ambitions vigorously. Three to six months' worth of living expenditures should be saved in a liquid, readily accessible account.

9. Debt Management: If you have high-interest loans, such as credit card debt, consider debt reduction as a main aim. Paying off high-interest loans may free up resources for other goals.

10. Investment Strategy: Determine how your assets may assist you reach your objectives. Consider more aggressive investments with larger growth potential for long-term objectives like retirement. Choose more cautious investments for short-term aims to safeguard your wealth.

11. Budgeting: Make a precise budget including your income, spending, and savings contributions. Your budget is a tool that can

assist you in successfully allocating finances toward your goals.

12. Regular Review: Review your financial goals on a regular basis and alter them as needed. Because life conditions vary, so should your aspirations.

13. Professional Advice: If you're confused about investing methods, retirement planning, or sophisticated financial objectives, consider speaking with a financial adviser for professional advice.

14. Maintain Motivation: Keep your goals in mind to remain motivated. Visualize the advantages of accomplishing them and remind yourself why they are important to you.

15. Celebrate Milestones: Commemorate your accomplishments along the route. Reaching milestones, no matter how little, may bring inspiration and a feeling of success.

16. Maintain Consistency: Maintaining consistency is essential. Maintain your financial strategy even when presented with problems or temptations to divert from your goals.

Establishing financial goals gives you a road map for your financial path. It assists you in making educated choices and taking intentional activities to achieve a more secure and profitable financial future.

Part I: Establishing a solid financial foundation

3. Making a financial plan

Making a financial strategy

Establishing a sound financial foundation is critical for long-term financial stability and success. A thorough financial plan may provide you direction, control, and peace of mind. In this part, we will look at the important processes involved in Establishing a sound financial foundation by Making a financial plan.

1. Evaluate Your Current Financial Situation: In this stage, you will examine your income, spending, assets, and obligations in depth. You may acquire a full grasp of where you are financially by examining your financial status. This examination assists you in identifying areas

for development, such as cutting needless costs or boosting your revenue. It also enables you to create achievable objectives depending on your present financial situation.

2. Establish Financial objectives: Establishing clear financial objectives is essential for developing a road map to success. These objectives should be SMART (specific, measurable, attainable, relevant, and time-bound). For example, you may want to save a certain amount for retirement by a given age, pay off a certain debt by a certain date, or save for a down payment on a property. By identifying your objectives, you give your financial path direction and purpose.

3. Make a Budget: A budget is an essential tool for managing your income and spending. It entails analyzing and classifying your sources of income as well as allocating monies to several spending categories such as housing, utilities, transportation, food, entertainment, and savings. A budget allows you to guarantee that your costs

match your income, make appropriate modifications to prevent overspending, and allocate monies to achieve your financial objectives.

4. Create an Emergency Fund: Because life is unpredictable, having an emergency fund is essential. An emergency fund is a financial safety net for unforeseen needs such as medical bills, job loss, or costly auto repairs. Set up three to six months of living costs in a separate savings account. This liquid savings buffer gives you piece of mind and keeps you from having to depend on high-interest credit cards or loans during difficult times.

5. Manage and Reduce Debt: Debt management and reduction are critical components of having a sound financial foundation. Begin by arranging your debts, which should include credit card balances, loans, and mortgages. Prioritize debts with higher interest rates and seek debt consolidation or balance transfer techniques to reduce interest payments. Create a debt

repayment strategy that works for you and commit to making regular payments. Paying down debt progressively frees up more of your income for savings and investment.

Saving and investing are important components of long-term financial stability. Make saving a habit by automating monthly contributions to a savings account, whether for short-term objectives such as a trip or long-term goals such as a housing down payment. Consider investing in retirement accounts, such as a 401(k) or an individual retirement account (IRA), to benefit from tax advantages and the power of compound interest. As your financial condition improves, look into other investing opportunities that match your risk tolerance and financial objectives.

7. Protect Your Financial Future: Protecting your financial future entails having enough insurance coverage. Health insurance protects you from large medical bills, while life insurance protects your loved ones financially in the case of your

death. Unexpected car repairs or house damage are covered by auto and homeowner's insurance. Analyze your insurance requirements, examine your current policies, and get expert advice to ensure you have enough coverage to safeguard your possessions and loved ones.

By taking these actions, you may lay a strong financial foundation and move toward long-term financial stability and success. Remember that financial planning is a continual process that involves constant monitoring, modifications, and adaptation in order to keep up with life changes and economic situations.

4. Managing Your Debts

Debt management is a vital component of establishing a healthy financial foundation. You may minimize financial stress, boost your creditworthiness, and generate more prospects for long-term financial stability by efficiently managing your obligations. Let's go further into this topic.

1. Assess Your Present Debt Situation:
Begin by conducting a thorough inventory of your current obligations. Credit card debt, loans, mortgages, and any other outstanding liabilities are all included. Make a list of all your debts, including the outstanding amount, interest rate, minimum payment, and due date. This evaluation will assist you in understanding your total debt load and prioritizing your repayment plan.

2. construct a Debt payback Plan: Once you've identified your debts, construct a debt payback plan. Begin by categorizing your debts according to characteristics such as interest rates or outstanding sums. You may want to prioritize high-interest debts in order to reduce the amount of interest you pay over time. Alternatively, you might use the "snowball method" to create momentum and drive by focusing on minor debts first.

3. Set aside Enough Money for Debt Repayment:

Determine how much you can put aside each month for debt reduction. Look for places in your budget where you might decrease spending and devote those dollars to debt repayment. Consider temporarily adopting a modest lifestyle to expedite your debt payback process. As indicated in the last section, creating a budget might assist free up more income for debt repayment.

4. Negotiate with Creditors: If you are having difficulty making debt payments, contact your creditors. They may be ready to negotiate lower interest rates, alter repayment arrangements, or even settle for a smaller sum in certain situations. Communicating with your creditors and clarifying your financial circumstances might assist you in finding mutually beneficial solutions and easing some of the pressure.

5. Avoid Taking on New Debt: While working to pay off current debt, it's critical to avoid taking on new debt. Maintain sensible spending habits and be aware of your financial constraints. To avoid excessive debt, consider utilizing cash or debit cards instead of credit cards. Develop sound financial practices that are in line with your long-term objectives to avoid falling into the trap of borrowing more than you can reasonably repay.

6. Seek Professional Advice if Necessary: If you're feeling overwhelmed by your debt situation or want specialist advice, consider consulting with a financial counselor or debt management pros. They may give customised plans, negotiate with creditors on your behalf, and provide useful information to assist you in properly managing your debt.

You may take charge of your financial circumstances and build a strong financial foundation by aggressively controlling your debt. Implementing a debt repayment plan, allocating enough finances for repayment, communicating with creditors, and avoiding new debt can put you on the road to long-term financial security. To attain the financial independence you want, remember that controlling your debt involves dedication, discipline, and constant monitoring.

5. Emergency funding

Creating an emergency fund is a critical component of building a sound financial foundation. Having a separate fund for unforeseen needs gives financial protection as well as peace of mind. Let's take a closer look at the notion of emergency finance.

1. The Importance of an Emergency Fund: An emergency fund acts as a financial safety net in the event of an unanticipated event such as a medical emergency, job loss, or costly house repairs. It serves as a cushion to keep you from depending on credit cards, loans, or other types of high-interest debt during difficult times.

Building an emergency fund is critical for preserving your financial security and avoiding the derailment of long-term financial objectives.

2. Determine the Optimal Size of Your Emergency Fund: Aim to save three to six months of living costs in your emergency fund. Consider your monthly costs, the consistency of your income source, and any possible dangers in your life. If you have dependents or are facing more uncertainty, you should save at the upper end of the spectrum. However, any amount saved is advantageous and gives some degree of security.

3. Prioritize Emergency Fund Contributions: Make regular contributions to your emergency fund a priority. To achieve continuous savings, treat it as a fixed item in your budget. If you have a limited budget, begin by establishing modest savings goals and progressively increasing the amount over time. Set up automatic payments from your checking account

to your emergency fund to make saving easy and consistent.

4. Keep Your Emergency Fund distinct from Other Accounts: Keep your emergency fund distinct from your regular checking account and any other savings accounts you may have. This distinction guarantees that you do not inadvertently use the money for non-emergency costs. Consider creating a second high-yield savings account that allows you to easily access your assets while still collecting a small amount of interest.

5. Flexibility and replenishment: An emergency fund should be adaptable. While it is generally intended for unforeseen occurrences, it may also be utilized for anticipated costs or opportunities. However, avoid completely depleting the money and always seek to restore it as quickly as possible following any withdrawals.

6. store Your Emergency Fund Liquid: Because the aim of an emergency fund is to offer rapid

access to cash when required, store the money in low-risk liquid assets. Avoid investing your emergency money in long-term investments or assets that may incur fines or losses if used early. Keep in mind that the aim is to have the required finances on hand in case of an unanticipated crisis.

7. Gradually Increase the amount of Your Emergency Fund: As your financial journey progresses, consider gradually increasing the amount of your emergency fund to give more padding. Examine your lifestyle, financial obligations, and any changes that may affect your monthly spending. Adjust your savings objectives to ensure your emergency fund maintains up with your changing demands.

You may shield yourself from unforeseen financial problems and develop a sound financial foundation by actively establishing and maintaining an emergency fund. A substantial emergency fund gives you the confidence to manage tough times, decreases your dependence on debt, and keeps you on pace to meet your financial objectives. Remember that investing your emergency fund needs discipline, consistency, and a long-term outlook to ensure you are fully prepared for any unforeseen financial issues that may happen.

Part II: Investing

6. Simple investing

Simple Investing gives people the chance to enhance their money over time. It entails investing money in different financial products such as stocks, bonds, real estate, or mutual funds in order to obtain a return on investment.

Simple investing focuses on tactics that are simple to comprehend and use, making it suitable for novices or those who want a hands-off approach. The idea is to build a portfolio that balances risk and possible returns.

The notion of long-term investment is a core component of simple investing. Rather of attempting to timing the market or participate in frequent trading, it focuses on keeping assets for a lengthy period of time. This strategy permits investments to develop consistently over time while also mitigating the effect of short-term market swings.

Diversification is another important part of basic investment. Individuals may lessen the risk associated with putting all of their eggs in one basket by diversifying their assets across asset classes and sectors. Diversification mitigates the risk of losses from a single investment or area.

Because of their diversification and reduced expense ratios, low-cost index funds and exchange-traded funds (ETFs) are often preferred in basic investment methods. These funds give investors with quick diversification by giving exposure to a diverse choice of equities or bonds without the need for substantial research or continuous management.

Simple investing requires investors to prioritize their financial objectives and risk tolerance. Individuals may coordinate their investing decisions by setting a clear investment aim and recognizing their risk tolerance levels.

Even with a basic investment strategy, researching and being educated on the principles of investing is critical. Understanding fundamental principles like asset allocation, risk management, and the power of compounding will help you make more educated financial choices.

Finally, it is critical to analyze and appraise the investment portfolio on a regular basis. Monitoring investment performance and making modifications as needed ensures that the portfolio stays aligned with changing market circumstances and individual objectives.

To summarize, simple investing is a plain and approachable method of building money over time. Individuals may traverse the world of investing with confidence and perhaps attain their financial goals by concentrating on long-term strategies, diversification, and low-cost funds.

7. Investing in Stocks

Stock investing may be an interesting and possibly rewarding method to enhance your money. However, it is critical to approach it with awareness and caution. In this post, we will take a deep dive into stock investing, studying the important principles and tactics that may help you make educated stock market selections.

Understanding Stocks: Before beginning to invest, it is essential to understand the fundamental notion of stocks. Stocks are purchased and traded on stock markets to reflect ownership in a firm. Investors who buy stocks become shareholders and have a stake in the company's revenues and losses.

Starting Out:
To begin investing in stocks, you must first determine your financial objectives and risk tolerance. Determining your investment horizon, or the length of time you want to keep the

stocks, will also influence your investing approach.

Research and knowledge are essential for successful stock market investment. Understanding the larger economic climate, examining market patterns, and studying financial reports are all important elements in making educated investment choices. You may improve your knowledge of the firms you want to invest in by getting up to date on the latest news and studying from credible sources.

Choosing Stocks: Choosing the appropriate stocks takes serious thought. Financial health of the organization, industry trends, competitive advantages, and managerial competency all play a role. Fundamental analysis, which studies the company's financial statements and development prospects, and technical analysis, which examines stock price patterns and market movements, are two popular methods for evaluating equities.

Diversification is an important risk management approach in investing. Spreading your investment over a diverse range of companies from several sectors helps to mitigate the influence of any one company's performance on your total portfolio. If one stock underperforms, the others may balance the loss, lowering risk.

Risks and Rewards: Investing in stocks has some risks. Stock prices may change dramatically owing to a variety of variables such as market circumstances, geopolitical events, company-specific news, or economic phenomena. It is critical to be prepared for short-term volatility while maintaining a long-term perspective. The stock market has historically produced better returns than other investing options, but previous performance does not guarantee future outcomes.

Building a Portfolio: Having a well-diversified portfolio may help you achieve long-term success. To develop a portfolio that matches with their objectives and risk tolerance, investors might examine several investment strategies such as growth investing, value investing, or a mix of both. It is important to examine and rebalance your portfolio on a regular basis to ensure that it stays consistent with your investing goals.

Monitoring and Patience: It is critical to monitor your investments and keep track of the success of your portfolio. Markets may be volatile, therefore it is critical to examine your investing thesis on a regular basis. When investing in stocks, patience is essential since short-term market changes may not necessarily represent a company's underlying worth. Focusing on long-term objectives and maintaining a disciplined approach will help you handle market swings.

Conclusion: Investing in equities offers potential for wealth building, but it takes knowledge, study, and a long-term outlook. Understanding the foundations of stock market investing, analyzing risks, diversifying your portfolio, and remaining educated may help you achieve your financial objectives. Remember that stock investing should be undertaken with caution and caution.

8. Bonds and Safe Investments

Bonds are less volatile than stocks since their value is determined by set interest payments and the repayment of capital at maturity. As a result, they are appealing to conservative investors that value capital preservation.

Bond revenue is distributed in the form of coupon payments. Coupons are interest payments paid by the bond issuer to the bondholder on a regular basis. These payments are often provided semi-annually or yearly, giving a consistent source of income.

The yield of a bond determines its rate of return. Various variables impact yield, including the issuer's credit rating, current interest rates, and the duration to maturity. Bonds with better credit ratings and longer maturities have higher yields in general.

Diversified bond portfolios may also assist to reduce risk. Individuals diversify their risk among multiple issuers, sectors, and maturities by investing in a range of bonds. This diversity mitigates the risk of a single bond or issuer defaulting.

Investors seeking secure investments and bonds should examine credit quality and term. Bonds issued by governments or highly rated firms are typically considered to be safer investments, but longer-term bonds may give larger yields but also involve a higher interest rate risk.

It is essential to remember, however, that While bonds are regarded reasonably secure investments, there is still some risk associated. Changes in interest rates, credit ratings, and economic conditions can all have an impact on bond pricing and returns.

Individuals should keep up to speed on market circumstances, interest rate trends, and the creditworthiness of bond issuers in order to make informed investing selections. Furthermore, before allocating cash to bonds or safe investments, it is critical to examine one's individual risk tolerance and investment objectives.

In conclusion, investing in bonds and secure assets allows individuals to conserve capital while generating consistent income. Bonds can be a significant component of a diversified portfolio for conservative investors seeking stability and consistent returns because to their lower volatility and regular coupon payments.

9. Spreading Your Money

The Art of Asset Allocation and Diversification

Diversifying your assets is a basic tenet of effective investing. Diversification is a technique that helps to control risk and enhance possible profits. In this post, we will look at the notion of spreading your money and the significance of diversification and asset allocation.

Understanding Diversification: Diversification is the practice of investing in a diverse group of assets or securities from various businesses, sectors, or geographies. The idea is to limit the influence of any one investment's performance on the total performance of your portfolio. Diversification reduces the risk of losing a large percentage of your investment if one asset or industry underperforms.

Benefits of Diversification: Diversification provides various advantages to investors, including:

1. Risk Management: Spreading investments helps to manage risks by lowering asset concentration in a single investment. If one item underperforms, others may compensate, offering a buffer to your portfolio.

2. prospective Returns: Diversification may boost prospective returns as well. You may balance high-risk/high-reward investments with more stable, lower-risk ones by investing in a mix of assets with varied risk profiles, thereby maximizing your total return over time.

3. Volatility Smoothing: Different assets often respond differently to market situations. A well-diversified portfolio may suffer reduced volatility since the ups and downs of individual assets may not have the same impact on the overall portfolio.

Asset Allocation is the strategic distribution of your investment portfolio across several asset classes such as stocks, bonds, cash, and alternative assets such as real estate or commodities. Determining the proper asset allocation is critical for building a well-balanced and diverse portfolio.

Considerations for Asset Allocation:
When choosing your asset allocation, keep the following considerations in mind:

1. Risk Tolerance: Your risk tolerance influences your asset allocation significantly. Conservative investors may invest more in bonds or cash, while aggressive investors may invest more in stocks or risky assets.

2. Investment Horizon: Asset allocation is influenced by the length of time you expect to retain assets. Long-term investors have greater time to ride out short-term market swings and may invest more in growth assets.

3. Financial Objectives: Your personal financial objectives, such as retirement planning, education savings, or house ownership, can assist drive your asset allocation selections. Different objectives may need varying amounts of risk and reward.

Rebalancing: Once you've determined your asset allocation, it's critical to examine and rebalance your portfolio on a regular basis. Market volatility might lead your investments to deviate from your initial allocation. Rebalancing your portfolio means returning it to its planned allocation by selling over-weighted assets and purchasing under-weighted ones. This method guarantees that your portfolio stays on track with your investing goals and risk tolerance.

Professional Advice and study: Investing and asset allocation are complicated processes that need meticulous analysis and study. Seeking financial counsel or completing extensive study on different investment possibilities may help you make smart asset allocation decisions.

Conclusion: Diversification and deliberate asset allocation are important strategies for minimizing risk and improving returns in investing. You might possibly lessen the effect of market volatility and increase your chances of meeting your financial objectives by diversifying your investment across multiple asset classes and industries. Remember to examine and rebalance your portfolio on a regular basis to ensure that it is consistent with your risk tolerance and goals.

10. **Real Estate and Other Investments**

In addition to standard stocks and bonds, investors may choose from a wide range of alternative investment choices. Real estate and other assets provide distinct diversity and possible profits. In this essay, we will look at the world of real estate and other investments, their rewards, and important factors to consider as investors.

Real estate investments have long been seen as a tangible and meaningful financial choice. Investing in real estate has a number of benefits, including:

1. Potential Appreciation: Real estate has the potential to appreciate over time, providing investors with financial gains.

2. Cash Flow: Rental properties may produce consistent rental revenue, resulting in a consistent cash flow stream.

3. Diversification: Real estate provides diversification advantages by introducing a new asset class that acts differently from equities and bonds. It may assist in lowering the total risk of an investment portfolio.

4. Inflation Protection: Real estate assets, especially income-producing properties, may act as an inflation hedge. Rental income and property values typically grow when prices rise, protecting buying power.

Real Estate Investment Factors to Consider:
Investing in real estate takes careful consideration of many variables, including:

1. Location: A property's location has a substantial influence on its potential for appreciation and rental revenue. Neighborhood amenities, closeness to transit, career possibilities, and general economic development should all be considered.

2. Property Type: Different forms of real estate, such as residential, commercial, industrial, or mixed-use properties, each have their own set of benefits and drawbacks. Each sort of property has its own set of characteristics and market elements that should be recognized before investing.

3. Financing and Risk Management: Financing is often used in real estate ventures. Understanding financing choices, interest rates, and the dangers associated with leverage is critical for successful real estate investment.

Alternative Investments: In addition to real estate, alternative investments provide further diversity and possible rewards. Among these investments are:

1. Private Equity: Investing in private enterprises, frequently via venture capital or private equity funds, may give significant profits but also greater risks and longer holding periods.

2. Hedge Funds: Hedge funds use numerous investing methods to generate favorable returns, such as long/short equities, global macro, or event-driven. These funds are usually only accessible to qualified investors and have higher minimum investment requirements.

3. Commodities: Investing in commodities such as gold, silver, oil, or agricultural items may serve as an inflation hedge and diversify a portfolio.

4. Precious Metals: During times of economic instability, precious metals such as gold, silver, platinum, and palladium are often seen as safe-haven investments. They may serve as a

store of wealth and provide possible security against currency depreciation.

5. Cryptocurrencies: Although digital currencies such as Bitcoin and Ethereum have grown in popularity, they are more volatile and risky. Investing in cryptocurrencies requires extensive study and comprehension of the underlying technology and market dynamics.

Due Diligence and Professional Advice: Investing in real estate and alternative assets entails a number of complicated concerns. It is critical to do extensive due diligence, evaluate risk concerns, and comprehend the investment's liquidity and prospective returns. Seeking guidance from experienced specialists, such as financial advisers or real estate experts, may give significant insights and assist with risk mitigation.

Conclusion: Beyond standard stocks and bonds, real estate and alternative investments provide unique prospects for diversification and possible rewards. Real estate investing requires careful consideration of location, property type, and financing choices. Diversification may be further enhanced by investing in alternative assets such as private equity, hedge funds, commodities, precious metals, and cryptocurrencies. To make educated judgments in these investments, always undertake complete study, understand the dangers, and seek expert guidance.

Part III: Earning more money

11. Ways to earn extra money

When it comes to earning extra money, keep in mind that the effectiveness of these ideas will vary based on individual circumstances and the quantity of effort put into them. You have various options. Let's dig a little more into some of the concepts I addressed previously.

1. Freelancing entails giving your skills and services on a project-by-project basis. Identify your area of skill, whether it's writing, graphic design, photography, web development, or social media management, and establish a portfolio to exhibit your work. You can then discover clients by using freelancing websites or networking within your sector.

2. Online surveys or microtasks: Many websites and applications offer paid surveys or minor tasks like data entry or content moderation.

While the pay may not be considerable, it can be a simple and flexible method to earn extra money in your spare time.

3. Renting out your space: If you have a spare room, vacation property, or even a parking space, you may rent it out to visitors or those in need of temporary housing. Platforms such as Airbnb and VRBO make it easy to connect with potential renters and earn extra money.

4. Tutoring or teaching: If you excel in a particular area or have specialized expertise, you can give tutoring services or teach classes in person or online. There are places where you can sign up to connect with students that need help.

5. Pet sitting or dog walking: If you enjoy working with animals, consider giving pet sitting or dog walking services. Many pet owners are prepared to pay for dependable and trustworthy personnel to care for their furry pals.

6. Renting out your belongings: If you have products that are not commonly utilized, such as camera equipment, power tools, or party supplies, you can rent them out to others in your community. Using peer-to-peer rental networks can help you connect with potential renters.

7. Reselling goods: This entails locating discounted products in thrift stores, garage sales, or internet marketplaces and then reselling them for a profit. Platforms such as eBay or Facebook Marketplace can be excellent places to resell.

8. Virtual assistant work: Many individuals and businesses want assistance with administrative or organizing activities. As a virtual assistant, you can provide assistance in areas like as email management, scheduling, and customer support.

Remember that success in making extra money generally depends on your dedication, resourcefulness, and adaptability. It is critical to thoroughly examine and comprehend the legal and regulatory implications of any strategy you choose.

12. Starting your own business

Starting your own business may be a thrilling and rewarding experience. Here's a more detailed breakdown of the stages involved:

1. Identifying a Business Idea: Start by identifying a business idea that aligns with your interests, abilities, and market demand. Consider your interests, hobbies, and areas of skill as a starting point for developing ideas.

2. Research and Planning: Conduct market research to better understand your target audience, possible rivals, and product or service demand. This will assist you in identifying opportunities and fine-tuning your business plan. Make a detailed business plan outlining your objectives, tactics, financial predictions, and marketing strategy.

3. Legal and Financial Considerations: Decide on a legal structure for your firm, such as a sole proprietorship, partnership, or limited liability corporation (LLC), and register it with the proper authorities. To keep personal and corporate finances separate, open a separate business bank account. Determine how you will manage industry-specific taxes, licenses, permits, and insurance requirements.

4. Funding Your Business: Evaluate your financial requirements and investigate potential funding options. You have the option of funding the business yourself (bootstrapping), seeking investors, applying for small business loans, or using crowdfunding services.

5. Establish Your Infrastructure: Depending on the type of your business, establish a physical or virtual office space, purchase required equipment and supplies, and set up systems for accounting, payroll, inventory management, and customer relationship management.

6. Branding and Marketing: Create a strong brand identity, including a recognizable name, logo, and visual elements that are consistent. Make a marketing strategy to reach your target audience that includes both online and offline channels such as websites, social media, advertising, public relations, and networking.

7. Launch and Operations: Put your plans into action and officially launch your company. Ascertain that you have all of the relevant licenses and permits to operate legally. Monitor and alter your processes, product/service offerings, and customer experience on a regular basis to respond to market developments and feedback.

8. Financial Management: Maintain correct financial records, manage your income and expenses, and assess your financial performance on a regular basis. Prepare and monitor budgets, manage cash flow, and, if necessary, consult with an accountant or bookkeeper.

9. Expansion, diversification, and scaling up: As your company grows, look for chances for expansion, diversification, and scaling up. To remain competitive in the market, keep up with industry changes, engage in professional growth, and be open to changing your strategies.

Starting a business involves commitment, hard work, and tenacity. To boost your chances of success, surround yourself with mentors, seek professional guidance, and stay tuned in to the demands of your clients.

13. Earn money while you are sleep

Earning money while you sleep is known as passive income. While it may sound enticing, it is crucial to understand that creating truly passive income streams usually necessitates significant upfront labor and commitment. Here are a few ideas for earning money while you sleep:

1. Owning and renting out properties can provide rental revenue, allowing you to earn money even when you're not actively working. However, managing rental properties may necessitate the investment of time, resources, and skill.

2. Dividend stocks: Investing in dividend companies can provide a steady stream of income. You receive a percentage of the company's income in the form of dividends as a shareholder without actually working.

3. Royalties: You can receive royalties from sales or licensing agreements if you develop intellectual property, such as publishing a book, composing music, or designing items. This provides the possibility of continued income even after the first creation.

4. Online businesses: Creating an online business, such as e-commerce, affiliate marketing, or digital items, can provide passive income. Once created, these enterprises have the

ability to generate consistent revenue without the need for regular oversight.

5. Peer-to-peer lending: You can lend money to individuals or businesses through internet platforms and earn interest on the loans. While an initial investment is required, the interest generated can provide passive income over time.

While these approaches can generate revenue while you sleep, they still necessitate continual management and monitoring to assure the success and longevity of your passive income sources. Furthermore, before pursuing any investment or business opportunity, it is critical to undertake complete research, identify risks, and consider getting professional guidance.

Part IV: Getting ready for retirement

14. Retirement savings

Retirement savings is a financial strategy that aims to lay aside assets during your working years in order to support yourself in retirement when you no longer have a consistent income. It entails making monthly contributions to retirement accounts like IRAs or employer-sponsored plans like 401(k)s in order to build wealth over time.

Starting early is frequently suggested since it gives investments more time to develop through compounding interest. Small efforts given early on can add up to a lot over time. If you haven't started saving for retirement yet, it's never too late. Every little bit counts, and starting to save now is preferable to starting later.

When planning for retirement, it is critical to evaluate your personal financial condition, goals, and risk tolerance. Investigating various retirement savings choices, such as Roth IRAs or standard 401(k)s, will help you choose which pathways are best for you. Seeking counsel from a financial advisor can also help in developing a customized retirement savings strategy.

Regular payments are essential for establishing a retirement fund. Consistency is essential. Establish a budget and a plan to routinely contribute a percentage of your income to retirement savings. Contributions that are automated can make saving easier and more disciplined.

It is also critical to make sound financial decisions along the way. Examine your costs to see where you may cut back and channel those cash to retirement savings. Reduced high-interest debt and prudent investment management can also help your retirement savings grow.

Keep in mind that everyone's retirement savings goals will vary depending on their lifestyle preferences, intended retirement age, and post-retirement plans. As your circumstances change, it's critical to examine and adapt your retirement savings strategy on a regular basis. Keeping track of your financial status on a regular basis will help you to make any required modifications and guarantee you're on track to fulfill your retirement objectives.

Overall, retirement planning is a continuous process that necessitates discipline and intelligent decision-making. You may lay a firm foundation for a comfortable retirement by starting early, contributing consistently, and making wise financial decisions.

15. Retirement account and taxes

Retirement funds and their relevance to taxes.

Individual retirement accounts (IRAs) and employer-sponsored plans like 401(k)s are designed to help individuals save for retirement in a tax-efficient manner. These accounts provide a variety of tax advantages that can assist optimize savings over time.

Traditional retirement account contributions are normally tax-deductible in the year they are made. This implies that your contribution reduces your taxable income for the year, potentially lowering your overall tax liability. For instance, if you put $5,000 to a regular IRA and earn $50,000, you may only be taxed on $45,000. Keep in mind, however, that there are annual contribution limits to these accounts.

Investment growth and earnings in retirement accounts are tax-deferred. This implies that any interest, dividends, or capital gains earned within the account are tax-free until you withdraw the assets in retirement. This can be advantageous since it permits investments to possibly develop faster because taxes are not deducted immediately.

It is crucial to understand, however, that withdrawals from typical retirement accounts in retirement are subject to ordinary income tax. This means you'll have to pay taxes on the amount you withdraw, based on your tax bracket at the time. To understand the tax implications of your unique retirement account and withdrawal strategy, speak with a tax professional or financial counselor.

Roth retirement accounts, on the other hand, are funded using after-tax monies, which means that contributions are not tax deductible. The advantage comes after retirement, when withdrawals from a Roth account are usually tax-free. This means you won't have to pay taxes on the account's growth or earnings, or on eligible withdrawals in retirement.

When it comes to taxes and retirement accounts, it's critical to understand the rules and restrictions that are unique to each type of account. Furthermore, tax regulations vary over time, so it's critical to stay up to date and contact with a tax specialist or financial counselor as needed.

Overall, retirement accounts provide tax benefits that can help people save for retirement more effectively. Individuals can optimize their savings and potentially minimize their tax burden during retirement by taking advantage of these tax breaks.

16. Making money last in retirement

Let's delve more into how to keep your money working for you in retirement:

1. Establish a thorough retirement budget. Carefully assess your anticipated outgoings in retirement, including essential living expenses, healthcare, travel, and recreation. Create a thorough budget that fits your lifestyle and sources of money.

2. Investigate other income sources: Relying entirely on one source of money could be problematic. Think about a variety of sources of income, including Social Security, pensions, rental income, part-time employment, and investment dividends. A more steady and constant cash flow may result from this.

3. Reduce debt to a minimum: Financial stress can be considerably decreased by retiring with little or no debt. You can use more of your retirement income if you pay off high-interest obligations like credit cards and mortgages.

4. Create a sustainable withdrawal strategy: To make sure your retirement savings last throughout your retirement years, figure out a safe withdrawal rate. The 4% rule is a widely used principle, albeit it is not infallible. In the first year of retirement, it advises taking withdrawals equal to 4% of your initial portfolio balance, with subsequent years' withdrawals being adjusted for inflation. However, specific

situations may call for a different withdrawal plan, therefore it's advisable to speak with a financial counselor.

5. Budget for healthcare bills: Medical costs typically increase as people age. Consider acquiring enough health insurance, and research Medicare choices. Including healthcare bills in your budget can enable you to plan ahead and prevent unforeseen financial hardships.

6. Keep an investment portfolio that is well-diversified: A well-diversified investment portfolio can lower risk and boost long-term returns. Based on your risk appetite and financial objectives, distribute your investments among a variety of assets, including stocks, bonds, and real estate. Maintain the alignment of your portfolio with your goals by reviewing and rebalancing it frequently.

7. Keep a tight check on your money throughout retirement and make necessary adjustments to your strategy. Review your investments

frequently, take into account any changes in your situation, and modify your plans as necessary. Being proactive can assist you in making wise choices and preserving your financial stability.

8. Be ready for unforeseen costs: Set up an emergency fund to cover unforeseen costs. Having a cash reserve can help you weather unforeseen financial difficulties and save you from prematurely withdrawing from your retirement resources.

9. Seek expert counsel: Think about hiring a financial advisor with experience in retirement planning. They may offer you individualized advice, assist you in weighing your options, and help you decide according to your particular circumstances.

Keep in mind that making your money last in retirement necessitates continuous assessment and modification. Keep track of any changes to tax rules and regulations, regularly review your financial strategy, and be ready to make adjustments as necessary. You can maintain your financial stability and have a comfortable retirement by being proactive.

Part V: Money security

17. How insurance can help

Insurance can play an important part in retirement planning by providing financial protection against unforeseen catastrophes. Here's a more detailed description of how insurance can assist:

1. Health Insurance: Healthcare costs rise in retirement, so having enough health insurance coverage is critical. Medicare is a government health insurance program for those over the age of 65 that covers a variety of medical treatments. It protects seniors from high medical costs and gives them access to vital healthcare. Supplemental insurance, such as Medigap policies or Medicare Advantage plans, can improve coverage while also lowering expenses.

Long-term care services, such as nursing homes, assisted living facilities, or home healthcare, can be costly. Long-term care insurance can help protect your retirement assets by covering these services if you require assistance with daily chores. It can help to ease financial burdens while also providing options for high-quality care.

3. Life Insurance: Life insurance can be used for a variety of purposes in retirement planning. As an example:

- Income Replacement: If you have dependents or debts that might create a financial strain on your loved ones, life insurance can give a death benefit to help replace lost income or cover outstanding financial commitments.
- Estate Planning: Life insurance can also be utilized to leave a legacy or provide recipients with an inheritance. It can assist in ensuring that your loved ones are financially sustained even after your death.
- Final Expenses: Life insurance can assist pay for funeral and burial expenses,

relieving your family of these financial burdens.

Annuities are insurance products that can provide a consistent income stream throughout retirement. They function by transforming a one-time payment into a series of payments over a set length of time or for the rest of your life. Annuities can assist provide stability and supplement other retirement income sources.

5.   Homeowners/Renters Insurance: In retirement, protecting your property from unexpected incidents such as fire, theft, or natural disasters is critical. Damage to your property or personal items is covered by homeowners or renters insurance. It can assist you in recovering financially in the event of an unpleasant situation.

6. Liability Insurance: Liability insurance, such as umbrella insurance, protects you from potential lawsuits or claims for personal harm or property damage made against you. It adds

financial protection above and above the liability limits of your underlying policies, such as home or auto insurance.

7. Disability Insurance: While disability insurance is commonly linked with protection against income loss while working, it can also be useful in retirement planning. It replaces your income if you become incapacitated and are unable to work. If you become disabled, disability insurance can help you secure your retirement assets and maintain your level of life.

When it comes to retirement insurance, it's critical to examine your unique needs, taking into account your health, financial goals, and personal circumstances. Consulting with an insurance specialist or financial advisor can assist you in evaluating your alternatives, determining the appropriate coverage levels, and ensuring that your insurance plans correspond with your retirement objectives.

18. Future planning

Future planning entails making deliberate decisions and taking action now to prepare for what is to come. It is a methodical strategy to achieving one's personal, financial, or professional objectives. Here is a more detailed description of future planning:

1. Goal Setting: Setting clear and defined goals is the first step in future planning. Determine your goals in several aspects of your life, such as finances, profession, relationships, health, and personal development. Setting objectives gives you direction and helps you prioritize your efforts toward your desired outcomes.

2. Financial Planning: Creating a financial roadmap is a common part of future planning. This includes budgeting, controlling income and expenses, saving for short- and long-term goals, and investing properly. It also includes retirement planning, insurance coverage, estate planning, and other financial issues. A

well-crafted financial plan assists you in laying a strong foundation for the future.

3. Career Development: Career growth and development are included in future planning. Setting career objectives, learning new skills, pursuing professional development opportunities, networking, and researching career progression chances are all examples of this. You may position yourself for success in the future employment market by planning for career progression and remaining adaptive.

4. Personal Development: Personal growth and self-improvement are equally important aspects of future planning. Setting personal objectives for self-care, physical health, emotional well-being, and lifelong learning may be part of this. Personal growth can help you live a more fulfilling and balanced life.

5. Risk Management: Future planning also includes recognizing potential risks and developing risk-mitigation methods. This

includes assessing potential threats to your objectives, such as economic downturns, unexpected events, health concerns, or natural disasters. Risk management methods such as emergency money, insurance coverage, and estate preparation can assist protect your future objectives.

6. Adaptability and Flexibility: Future planning understands the need to alter goals in response to changing conditions. Unexpected possibilities or obstacles may arise in the future, and flexibility is required to negotiate these situations. Reviewing, reassessing, and revising your plans on a regular basis will help ensure alignment with your changing needs and objectives.

7. continual Evaluation and Alignment: Planning for the future is a continual activity. It necessitates monitoring your progress toward your goals on a regular basis, determining if adjustments are required, and realigning your actions to keep on track. Regular evaluation and

course correction can help you stay focused and make the best decisions to reach your goals.

Remember that future planning is an ongoing activity. Proactive decision-making, discipline, and an open mind are required. You can strive toward a future that matches with your desires and leads to personal fulfillment by making clear goals, managing your finances, growing your talents, and adapting to changes.

19. Dealing with financial difficulties

Financial issues can be a difficult and stressful position to deal with. It can be caused by a variety of circumstances, including job loss, excessive debt, or unanticipated expenses. When confronted with financial challenges, it is critical to maintain a cool and sensible demeanor.

To begin, you should assess your present financial status. This involves figuring up your income, spending, and any outstanding debts. Making a budget will help you obtain a better grasp of your financial commitments and how much money you can afford to set aside for necessities and debt repayment.

Following that, you may need to make some changes to your lifestyle and spending habits. Reduce non-essential spending and look for ways to save money, such as cooking at home, using coupons or discounts, or looking for cheaper alternatives for particular services or items. It is also prudent to avoid incurring additional debt during this time period.

If you are having difficulty meeting your financial responsibilities, you should contact your creditors or lenders to discuss viable options. They could be prepared to work out a payment plan or provide interim respite to help you get back on track. In addition, consulting with a financial counselor or a debt reduction service can provide useful direction and aid in managing your financial issues.

While dealing with financial issues, it is critical to be proactive and maintain a positive outlook. Keeping a strong focus on your goals and practicing fiscal discipline will help you overcome these obstacles. Remember that financial challenges are frequently transient, and you may try to improve your financial condition with patience, determination, and help.

Part VI: financial independence

20. The Desired freedom

Desired freedom differs from person to person because it is subjective and very personal. It is the ability to live one's life according to one's own choices and values, without being constrained by external pressures or constraints.

For some, desired freedom may include the capacity to pursue one's passions and aspirations, to make decisions autonomously and independently, or to travel and see the globe. It can also entail the ability to express oneself authentically without fear of being judged or subjected to cultural pressure.

Desired freedom may include features such as political freedom, social equality, and the right to live in a just and inclusive society, in addition to personal freedom. It can include the right to express oneself and participate in the political process, as well as the right to be free from discrimination and oppression.

Finally, the depth of desired freedom is determined by each individual's particular vision and desires. It is a comprehensive term that reflects each person's particular values, experiences, and aspirations for a satisfying and meaningful life.

21. Staying on track

Maintaining attention and adherence to a given goal, task, or path in order to make progress and accomplish desired objectives is referred to as staying on track. It entails remaining focused, disciplined, and structured in order to avoid distractions, overcome difficulties, and remain committed to the desired course of action.

To go more into the concept of keeping on course, consider the following:

1. Clarity of Purpose: Understanding the aim or work at hand, as well as the desired consequence, provides motivation and helps you stay focused.

2. Goal Setting: It is critical to set clear, explicit, and attainable goals. Breaking down larger goals into smaller, doable activities keeps you on track and ensures you make progress.

3. Prioritization: Identifying and prioritizing tasks based on their relevance and urgency is critical for maintaining concentration and successfully allocating time and resources.

4. Self-Discipline: Developing discipline entails developing self-control, motivation, and resilience. To keep focused on the task at hand, you must avoid temptations, procrastination, and distractions.

5. Time Management: Making calendars, setting deadlines, and allocating time to certain tasks are all part of effective time management. It aids in

the avoidance of time-wasting activities and the maintenance of productivity.

6. Adaptability: As circumstances change, staying on track may necessitate adaptability and flexibility. To overcome problems and stay focused, it is necessary to be able to alter plans, methods, or approaches while remaining aligned with the end goal.

7. Accountability and Monitoring: Holding oneself accountable and analyzing progress on a regular basis aids in staying on track. Regularly monitoring and reviewing one's performance allows for the identification of areas for improvement and the implementation of necessary changes.

8. Resilience: Staying on course frequently necessitates dealing with setbacks, challenges, or failures. It is critical to develop resilience and bounce back from setbacks in order to stay motivated, learn from mistakes, and keep moving forward.

Individuals can build techniques and habits to improve attention, productivity, and goal achievement in various facets of their lives by deeply comprehending the complexities of keeping on track.

22. Leaving a financial legacy

Planning and preparing to pass on wealth or assets to future generations or causes that you care about is part of leaving a financial legacy. It includes the purposeful intention to leave a lasting impact on the financial well-being of your successors or the greater community, in addition to just accumulating riches during your lifetime.

Consider the following aspects to go more into the topic of leaving a financial legacy:

1. Wealth building: Creating a financial legacy frequently begins with careful wealth building. Saving, investing, and making sensible financial

decisions can all help you expand your assets over time.

2. Estate Planning: Estate planning is a vital component of leaving a financial legacy. This includes preparing a will, establishing trusts, and naming beneficiaries to guarantee that your assets are transferred in accordance with your preferences after your death.

3. Intergenerational Wealth Transfer: Typically, leaving a financial legacy entails passing wealth on to future generations, such as children or grandchildren. This could include monetary inheritances, real estate, or enterprises.

4. Charitable Giving: Leaving a financial legacy can include charitable causes or organizations that correspond with your ideals in addition to familial beneficiaries. Philanthropy allows you to make a difference in society long after you are gone.

5. Financial Education: Instilling financial knowledge and literacy in your heirs may be part of leaving a financial legacy. Educating them on good money management, investing, and appropriate financial habits will help ensure that the wealth you leave behind is preserved and grown.

6. Legacy Planning: Leaving a financial legacy can involve non-monetary components such as passing on family values, traditions, and wisdom, in addition to financial matters. This could include writing down family histories, anecdotes, or personal philosophies to pass down to future generations.

7. Legacy influence: Considering the influence on others is an important component of leaving a financial legacy. It is not only about the money, but about the great impact and long-term legacy it can leave for the recipients and the community at general.

Individuals may refine their plans, make educated decisions, and ensure the enduring effect of their riches, values, and accomplishments in the lives of their loved ones and society by delving further into these aspects of leaving a financial legacy.

Conclusion

23. Your Personal Road to Financial Independence

Sure, I can give you a general outline of the path to financial freedom. Financial independence is defined as having enough wealth and resources to maintain oneself without relying on traditional employment income. Here are the essential steps:

1. Establishing Financial Goals: Begin by establishing specific financial goals that reflect your values and aspirations. Having well-defined goals will help guide your financial decisions, whether it's saving for retirement, paying off debt, or investing in real estate.

2. Budgeting and Saving: Make a budget to keep track of your earnings and expenses. You'll be able to commit more money to your financial goals if you constantly analyze your spending

habits and discover areas where you can cut down or save.

3. Emergency Fund: Create an emergency fund with at least 3-6 months of living expenses. This safety net will shield you from unforeseen financial losses and provide you with peace of mind.

4. Debt Management: Evaluate your debts and devise a strategy for managing and paying them off efficiently. Begin by prioritizing high-interest debts and investigate debt-repayment tactics such as the debt snowball or debt avalanche.

5. Investing: Begin investing your savings to gradually increase your fortune. Understand the various investment options available, such as stocks, bonds, real estate, or mutual funds, and create a diversified investment portfolio that meets your risk tolerance and financial objectives.

6. Lifelong Learning: Learn about personal financial and investing methods. To stay informed about economic trends and investing prospects, read books, attend seminars, or visit reliable financial websites.

7. Earn More Money: Look for ways to earn more money, whether through career promotion, side hustles, or passive income streams. Increasing your earning potential can help you get closer to financial independence.

8. decrease spending: To improve your financial perspective, constantly assess and decrease unneeded spending. Consider downsizing, reducing discretionary spending, and figuring out how to live frugally without sacrificing quality of life.

9. Plan for Retirement: Create a retirement plan that is in line with your financial objectives. Contributing as much as possible to retirement accounts such as 401(k)s or IRAs, as well as evaluating options such as company matching

programs or pensions, will help secure a pleasant retirement.

10. Review and Adjust: Review your progress on a regular basis and make any necessary adjustments to your financial strategy. Because life situations and economic conditions can change, it is critical to be proactive and adaptable on the path to financial independence.

Remember that gaining financial independence is a long-term process that necessitates discipline, perseverance, and dedication to your objectives. It is critical to maintain concentration, endure through difficulties, and seek professional advice when necessary.

www.ingramcontent.com/pod-product-compliance
Lightning Source LLC
Chambersburg PA
CBHW061002260726

48661CB00005B/1995